The Litt

CHAOS

The Little Book of
CHAOS

·

Craig Brown

Riverhead Books
New York

Riverhead Books
Published by The Berkley Publishing Group
A division of Penguin Putnam Inc.
375 Hudson Street
New York, New York 10014

First published in Great Britain by Warner Books in 1998.
First Riverhead trade paperback edition: June 1999

The Penguin Putnam Inc. World Wide Web site address is
http://www.penguinputnam.com

Library of Congress Cataloging-in-Publication Data

Brown, Craig.
    The little book of chaos / Craig Brown. — 1st Riverhead trade
pbk. ed.
        p.   cm.
    Originally published: Great Britain : Warner Books, 1998.
    ISBN 1-57322-759-5
    1. Life skills—Humor. 2. Conduct of life—Humor. I. Title.
PN6231.L48B76   1999
828'.91402—dc21
                                                        98-56277
                                                             CIP

Printed in the United States of America

10 9 8 7 6 5 4 3 2 1

For Frances

I've penned this little book to be a
source of much irritation to you
and your friends.
Keep it in your pocket at all times
and refer to it when calm threatens.

Those who follow its advice
will find themselves on edge.

And if they cannot irritate themselves
then at least they can irritate others.

Open this book
and step into a world
of petty grievance.

REGAIN THE CHILD WITHIN

The adult world is filled with tension.

Regain the child within.

Pull a colleague's hair.

RELAX

Help your partner relax.

Every ten minutes, say,

"RELAX!"

FENG SHUI

Move your bed over to the other

side of the room

and balance your mirror

on the window.

Place your rug over your lamp

and move the armchair across your door.

Now stay calm

until the ambulance arrives.

WEAR WHITE

The clothes you wear influence
your recollection of each passing day.

So wear white whenever you cook
and you will remember every ingredient
as day turns to night.

LIGHT A CANDLE IN YOUR BATH

Before climbing into your bath,

surround it

with bright flaming candles.

Some may set fire to the curtains;

others may scald your behind;

still others may fizzle out after a splash,

causing you much

vexation.

WELCOME A GOLDFISH

We can learn much
from the kingdom of the fish.
A goldfish brought home in a plastic bag
can teach us powers of observation
as it circles around aimlessly
before dying three months later
after you have left it behind
for a long weekend.

TAKE TIME WHEN
READING A MAP

When your partner is driving
along a highway,
wait until the car has just passed
the correct exit
before stating firmly,
"That was the right one."

CHAFE YOUR PRIVATE PARTS

In Chafe Therapy, garments of

100% nylon

are recommended for a complete chafing

of all your private parts.

INCREASE YOUR AWARENESS

Be aware of what is
going on at all times.
Before retiring to bed, tune into
CNN News for the latest update
of horrors around the world.

LIBERTY

Patience is a virtue
not easily acquired.
So when giving your boisterous nephew
a 1,000-piece jigsaw puzzle of
The Statue of Liberty,
first be sure to remove
the nose.

AN EFFECTIVE SUBSTITUTE

Out of sunblock?

Try mayonnaise.

HARKEN TO THE TUNE WITHIN

When all is silent around you, strive

to remember a tune that reached

number 17 in the charts in 1973.

Whistle half the chorus,

over and over again,

all day long.

Anyone who did not know the tune

will now know it

by heart.

PAMPER YOUR FEET

Spread jojoba oils on your feet.

Massage your feet with creams from

seven continents.

Pummel them with luxurious lotions.

Now put on your socks.

They will adhere to you wheresoever you

journey.

THE REWARD

Dieting?

Reward yourself at frequent intervals

with half-pound bars

of dairy milk chocolate.

YOUR DOG LOVES PEOPLE

Your dog loves people.

Let him demonstrate his affection

for your friends

by encouraging him to hump

their knees.

LIFE, TOO, IS CIRCULAR

Life is circular.

And so too is a roll of Scotch tape.

Always let the Scotch tape stick back

on itself between applications.

For by so doing, you will enjoy

the search for the lost end

and you will appreciate

that life, too, is circular.

WHEN TWO OR MORE ARE GATHERED

When two or more are gathered
around the TV set,
be sure to gain hold of the
remote control
and click it every three to four seconds.

THE PERFECT PICNIC

In search of the perfect place for a picnic?
Be sure to speed past the first seventeen sites
saying, "We can do better than that!"
At 2:50 P.M., you will realize that
the children are crying, the dog is dehydrated,
the cassettes have all melted
and the car is about to boil over.
"The perfect place!" you will exclaim,
as you drive into a field full of bulls.

SURPRISE!

Your dear friend has just turned fifty.

At last, she is eligible to join

The American Association of Retired Persons.

For that extra special birthday gift,

why not secretly fill out her application?

Surprise!

ONE NOTCH

Maintain your belt,
brassiere and buckled shoes
one notch too tight
to secure your discomfort
for the day ahead.

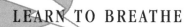

LEARN TO BREATHE

In the midst of office mayhem,
enrich your life by taking deep, deep
breaths.
Your colleagues will also benefit
from the sound
of your relaxation.

PIT YOUR WITS

Pit your wits against the vicissitudes
and vagaries of fortune by
remembering to set off between ten and
fifteen minutes late for those
urgent appointments.

FOR THE SAKE OF YOUR FELLOW PASSENGERS

When journeying on a train

keep in touch

by dialing your office

on your mobile phone

and bellowing,

loud and clear,

for the sake of your fellow passengers,

"Hi! I'm on a train!"

REMAINING ALERT

How to remain alert, even when
sipping a soothing mug of tea?
Find a broken mug.
Glue its handle back on.
Now, whenever you
sip tea from this cup
you will feel on red alert.

PRESENTS FOR THE KIDDIES

There is nothing like
a Mr. Microphone,
a drum kit or a karaoke machine
with a choice of
twenty-five different disco beats
to make your friends remember
exactly who gave their children
those presents.

A WELCOMING PLACE

Your fridge is a
welcoming place.
Fill it with many separate saucers
half-balanced on one another containing
four pieces of ravioli,
two spoonfuls of rice pudding,
a cracked egg and
eleven baked beans.

SLEEP LIKE A BABY

Sleep like a baby:

wake up every two to three hours

soaking wet

and bawling for food.

DAMP

Maintain a roll of damp toilet paper

for your visitors,

leaving them to ponder whether

it fell into

the toilet.

LEARNING TO CARE

If you are a doctor
or a health practitioner,
always remember
to refer to breasts as
boobs.

THE SPICE OF LIFE

Sick to death of the monotony

of the daily grind?

Lend variety to your footsteps

by placing gum

under your left sole.

POCKETS OF SURPRISE

Always be sure to carry four pairs of keys,

fifteen different coins,

a corkscrew, a lighter,

two discarded ring-pulls,

a metal dog whistle and three small spoons

distributed about your person

before passing through

the airport security gate.

FOUR SEASONS

While callers wait to be put through,

let them listen to

Vivaldi's *Four Seasons*.

COVER YOUR WOUND

Whenever you sustain an injury

take care

to use the type of adhesive bandage

that rips hairs from your skin

when you remove it

and leaves a dirty glue-like residue

for weeks after.

SOMEONE WE CAN LEAN ON

We all need someone we

can lean on.

So make sure you lean on

your partner

when walking up

a steep hill.

BE SURE

Distribute matchboxes
around your home.
But first be sure that they are filled
with spent matches.

LOYAL FRIENDS

Your friends have remained close by you

while you smoked cigarettes,

pipes and cigars,

while you broke wind and burped

and while you sang

"Bohemian Rhapsody."

But all is not lost.

Have you tried chewing tobacco?

CATCH YOURSELF

Catch yourself

unexpectedly

on a doorknob,

by wearing a dressing gown

with large bell sleeves.

A LITTLE CONSIDERATION

A little consideration
costs nothing.
When visiting a restaurant,
try to determine
how many sheets of paper
it takes to clog the toilet.
And then take pride
in reporting your findings
to the management.

AWAY FROM IT ALL

A little village in the Dordogne.

The office seems a million miles away.

But who's that waving hard at you

across the street?

Why, if it isn't

Frank from the fifth floor

and Maureen from accounting.

BEFORE LEAVING YOUR
PLACE OF WORK

Before leaving your place of work for

the weekend

be sure to set the burglar alarm

to ring

until your return.

SOAKING

When seeking to soothe away

the cares of the day,

climb into your bath

when it is still lukewarm,

immediately before

the hot water runs out.

Now remain where you are—

too chilly to get out,

too chilly to stay in.

SHOW YOUR SATISFACTION

When drinking beer,

always show your satisfaction

by going,

"Warrrgghhhhhh!"

and wiping your mouth with your sleeve.

MUCH TO LEARN

We have much to learn from other
animals.
In the height of summer, visit the
Everglades,
and learn much from
the little mosquito.

A NECESSARY ADDENDUM

Upon leaving the cinema,

while others are discussing

their favorite scenes,

remember to say,

"It wasn't nearly as good as the book."

AUTUMNAL HUES

Add an autumnal hue
to your armchair or sofa
by storing an apple core
down the side
and leaving it to
mature.

AFTER EACH DEEP SLEEP

After each deep sleep,

make a careful note of your

dreams

and recite them, in great detail,

to those you encounter,

always beginning,

"There was this, well, this

sort of *thing* . . ."

WHEN APPROACHED BY
A WEARY TRAVELER

When approached by a weary traveler

for directions,

take care to describe his route in the

greatest possible

detail

before adding,

"Actually, I've just thought of

a better way."

GO PLACIDLY

Go placidly into each noisy party,

always using your softest voice.

This way, those to whom you speak

will only catch every third word,

and they will feel obliged to interject,

"Really?"

to show that they understand

what on earth

you are talking about.

TO WELCOME A FRIEND

Before that special friend enters
your home,
prepare your children to give him or her
that extra-special welcome
by placing a Game Boy in their hands.

THE WORLD IS AT PEACE

A sunny day.

Happiness reigns.

The birds chirp in the trees.

Family and friends chat warmly.

The world is at peace with itself.

Why not ruin it all with a barbecue?

AN IMMUTABLE SIGN

Life leaves its own rich patina
upon your clothes.
Preserve these memories by taking your
clothes to a dry cleaners.
They will be returned looking exactly the same,
but now covered in safety pins,
and in labels saying,
WE HAVE BEEN UNABLE TO REMOVE
THESE STAINS COMPLETELY.

WATCH THE GRASS GROW

Purchase a lawn mower with a pull-start.

Pull. And pull. And pull. And pull. And
pull.

And pull. And pull. And pull. And pull.

Now collapse.

And watch the grass grow.

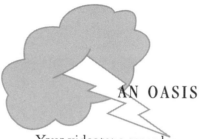

AN OASIS

Your videotape recorder provides an oasis

of chaos in a world riddled with calm.

Be sure to let its digital numbers flash

00.00

00.00

00.00

over and over and over again

throughout the day,

all day, everyday.

**GOING ANYWHERE NICE
THIS SUMMER?**

Pay a visit to your hairdresser

or to your dentist.

Sit back.

And wait for this question to be asked.

WHEN DRIVING THROUGH
A QUIET VILLAGE

When driving through a quiet village,
turn the volume of your new heavy metal CD
to its very highest:
CHUGGACHUGGACHUGGACHUGGA.
Then sit back, with a worldly expression
on your face
and slap your steering wheel knowingly
in time with the beat.

BLISS

For once, the kids are not squabbling.
They seem to have put all their feuds
and petty misunderstandings
behind them
Happiness reigns.
Bliss. Perfect bliss.
Monopoly, anyone?

DA-DA-DUM DUM DUM

Upon spying

a piano in a

friend's house,

be sure to play

the opening bars of "Chopsticks,"

over and over and over

and over and over

again.

THE JOURNEY OF LIFE

Leave no more than two minutes to buy
your bus ticket and stand behind the man
who wishes to find out the exact route,
times and price of a ticket
from Perth Amboy to Cape May,
taking in Paramus, East Stroudsburg,
Piscataway and Asbury Park,
using a Senior Citizen's discount coupon
that's two-and-a-half weeks out of date.

JINGLE, JANGLE

Chatting informally?
Let the world resound to the
jangling of loose change
in your trouser pockets.

TUCKING UP

A chilly night.

A warm bed.

You have finished a good book.

You sigh contentedly.

You switch off the light.

Peace. Perfect peace.

But did you remember to turn off the

oven?

GOOD OF YOU

The photos come back
from the developer.
Your friend stares at one in blank horror.
She looks
cross-eyed, red-faced, overweight and
close to death.
Reassure her by saying,
"That's good of you!"

A CAMPFIRE

No need for matches!

Just rub two sticks together for

half an hour

and

Hey Presto!

You will feel very hot.

A FRIENDLY NOTE

Employers!

Employ many people called John

in your place of work,

so that when you call one

the others all look up.

A TICKLE IN YOUR THROAT

A tickle in your throat?
Book the very best seat in the theater
and enjoy a good cough.

ADD INTEREST TO
YOUR PERSONALITY

Do people ignore you?
Why not cultivate a handlebar
moustache?
It could provide an invaluable
talking point.

THINK OF OTHERS

Always maintain a steady

40 mph

in the fast lane

so that your fellow drivers

are not tempted to break the speed limit.

A BESEECHING EYE

Never let a friend sit down
to eat
without placing a dog
at the corner of the table
to observe his every
mouthful
with a beseeching eye.

EVEN IN YOUR DARKEST HOURS

Though most commonly associated
with the 1970s,
Dr. Scholl's sandals are still widely available
in drugstores throughout the land.
Purchase a pair.
Their clackety noise will be your
companion,
even in your darkest hours.

THE INNER PERSON

A shiny metal ring strategically placed

through the bottom lip,

the tongue, the eyebrow or

the cheek,

will help bring out

the inner person.

KEEP IN TOUCH

Keep in touch with friends and acquaintances

by mailing them all a chain letter

beginning,

"Welcome to a marvelous opportunity!

Pedro aged thirty-three from Brazil

ignored this letter.

Just twelve days later, he died."

THE IMAGINATION IS A WONDERFUL THING

Before embarking on

a long journey,

take steps to tear the relevant

map

from your road atlas.

The imagination is a wonderful thing.

A WELCOME INTERRUPTION

It is 6:45 P.M. and all over the nation,
your fellow citizens are relaxing after
another hard day's work.
Some are chatting, others eating,
drinking or watching TV.
Now is the time to phone
and inform them they have been selected
for a once-in-a-lifetime special offer
on prestige double-glazing.

FOREVER FRESH

Before departing a friend's home,
remember to leave behind
your child's favorite teddy bear,
an urgent letter in an unstamped envelope,
a purse and a pair of hip waders.
As they gather them up,
wrap them, stamp them and post them,
the image of your face will remain
forever in their minds.

THE WAY TO HIS HEART

Paris in the spring.

You visit a bar, bustling with ordinary

French people, all ready with their orders.

Do not worry that you do not

know the language:

simply speak loudly to Le Patron

in pidgin English,

putting on a funny French accent

and gesticulating wildly.

A NEW UMBRELLA

Carry an umbrella with you
wheresoever you venture,
leave it behind, then
forget where you left it,
thus ensuring the need
to buy a new one.

THIRD FROM THE BACK

Your kid is in the chorus of his first school

musical.

Third row from the back, second from the left.

A moment to treasure for the rest of your days.

So be sure to position yourself

center stage

with your video camera

three-quarters of an hour before he comes on.

Your fellow parents will share your pride.

TWO THOUGHTFUL PRESENTS

Stuck for gift ideas for

two children of a friend?

Give one of them

a pet cat,

and the other

a pet mouse.

GREETING

Upon greeting a dear old friend

who's been through the wars,

look sympathetic and say,

"How are your spirits?

Low?"

THE GREEN BADGE OF COURAGE

Out on a first date?
Being interviewed for that important
new job?
A few skeins of spinach
stuck to the front teeth
will provide a reassuring badge
of identity.

THE TRUTH IS I NEVER LEFT YOU

Store managers!

Speed up your customers

by playing a light orchestral version of

"Don't Cry for Me Argentina"

over your crackly intercom.

LIVEN THINGS UP

If your dinner party begins to sag,
liven things up by reciting
the Monty Python Dead Parrot sketch
in a variety of amusing voices.

KEEP A SECRET

Say to a friend,

"I've got such an amazing secret

to tell you

but

I'd better not because I

promised I wouldn't."

GAS PUMP

When filling your car with gasoline

try to select a pump that

every few seconds

will click and stop pumping.

MAKE NEW FRIENDS

On moving to a
village or small country town,
make yourself known
to the close-knit community
by grabbing the front pew and
making sure you are
first up to communion.

TEENAGER?

You are aged?

Eighteen or under?

Be sure?

To add?

The interrogative?

To every?

Few words?

PHHPHHHWRAUUGHSNIFF-
SNIFFSNIFFPHWRAUGH

Friends and strangers alike
rejoice in the sound of
a nose well-blown.

ON A LONG JOURNEY

On a long journey with children,
say "McDonald's" within five minutes of
your departure.
Your children will enjoy lobbying you for
a Big Mac and french fries
for the next three and a half hours.

A NOVEL GIFT

Cheer up friends who have had

their house repossessed

by giving them a soothing present.

How about a

homing pigeon?

A SHARED ACTIVITY

When making love,
be sure to let your partner know
the joy you share.
Every now and then
laugh out loud.

SHARING

There is nothing so conducive to

friendship

as eating out and

splitting the cost.

Cement the friendship

by gazing at the bill,

getting out your calculator

and saying,

"But I didn't have any mineral water."

DEVOTION

Parking your car by a meter?
Feed the smallest amount into it,
thus ensuring you must return
at twelve-minute intervals.

A BORN RACONTEUR

Do you have a favorite

humorous anecdote

you like to repeat

toward the end of dinner parties?

Repeat it once every two months for the

next thirty years, and on 180 separate

occasions your partner will be reminded

that they are living with

a born raconteur.

AN ISLAND OF CALM

If a friend is

going mad

trying to find something,

be sure to remain an Island of Calm:

sit back in your chair,

sip gently at a cup of tea,

smile warmly and say,

"Now where did you last see it?"

THE KISS

Love does not arise without a struggle.

Kiss.

You suck; your partner sucks;

you both suck.

The dual-cyclone vacuum effect

stops you from breathing.

Only by suffering can we demonstrate

our love.

VISITING A FRIEND'S HOUSE

Everyone admires strength of character.

Whenever you visit a friend's house

for a meal

say, "Just a little for me—I'm on a diet,"

as the dish emerges from the oven.

BULLETIN

When asked,

"How are you?"

reply in full.

A WELCOME RESPONSE

When friends' children
refuse to eat what's on their plates,
lighten the atmosphere by exclaiming,
"I'm lucky! Mine eat everything!"

THE SECRET OF ETERNAL YOUTH

In the gap between two words

always insert

"Right?"

You have now gained the secret

of eternal youth.

THE PERFECT GUEST

When staying with a friend,
open and shut all the cupboards in
the kitchen.
When they say,
"What are you looking for?"
reply,
"Oh, don't worry, I'll soon find it."

CHEERING UP A FRIEND

Is your friend feeling a bit low?

Give her that

I've-just-won-the-Grand-Prix

sensation

by shaking a can of Coke

very hard before

handing it to her.

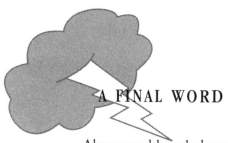

A FINAL WORD

Always read loosely bound

paperbacks,

so that when you are reaching their climax

and you turn over

the last-but-one page

you find

the last

sentence

doesn't

ABOUT THE AUTHOR

Craig Brown first came to prominence as the voice on the other end of the telephone that says, "Your call is important to us—please stay on the line." He is careful never to drive anywhere without leaving his right indicator flashing. He lives in Suffolk, England.

Email him on: .dot.craigbro.@.stresscenter.*.UK.scratchcard.@ stickysurfaces.imus.dot.exercisebike.@.dot.dot.dot.andonemoredot.